BLOOMFIELD TOWNSHIP PUBLIC LIBRARY

W9-BXE-197

Bloomfield Twp. Public Library
1099 Lone Pine Road
Bloomfield Hills, MI 48302-2410

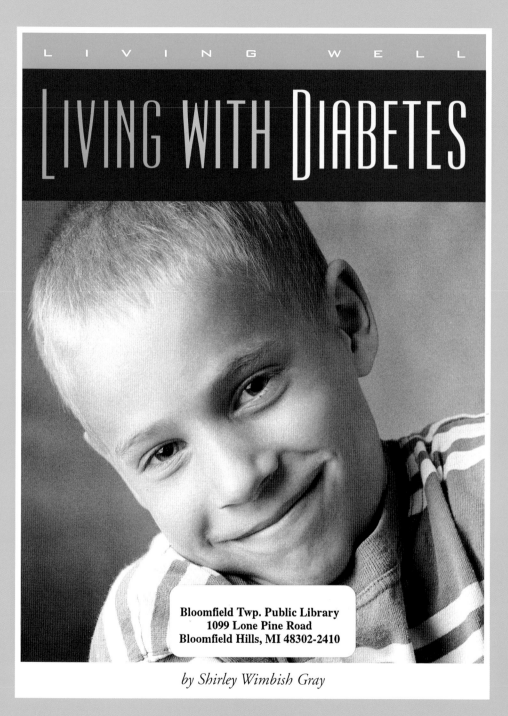

LIVING WELL

LIVING WITH DIABETES

Bloomfield Twp. Public Library
1099 Lone Pine Road
Bloomfield Hills, MI 48302-2410

by Shirley Wimbish Gray

THE CHILD'S WORLD®

CHANHASSEN, MINNESOTA

The Child's World

The publisher wishes to sincerely thank Maureen McGrath, R.N., C.P.N.P., C.D.E., for her help in preparing this book for publication.

Published in the United States of America by The Child's World®
P.O. Box 326
Chanhassen, MN 55317-0326
800-599-READ
www.childsworld.com

Photo Credits: Cover: Mark Andersen/RubberBall Productions, Custom Medical Stock Photo, Inc. (inset); Amy E. Conn/Associated Press: 19; Jim Rogash/Associated Press: 18; AFP/Corbis: 5; Roger Ressmeyer/Corbis: 15 (left); Reuters Newsmedia/Corbis: 21; Custom Medical Stock Photo, Inc.; 7, 9, 14 (both), 15 (right); Dan Dempster/ Dembinsky Photo Associates: 6; FPG International/GettyImages: 10, 11, 17, 23, 24; The Image Bank/GettyImages: 16, 22, 27; Stone/GettyImages: 20; Tony Freeman/ PhotoEdit: 8; Tom Prettyman/PhotoEdit: 12; David Young-Wolff/PhotoEdit: 13, 26; Mark Andersen/RubberBall Productions: 1

The Child's World®: Mary Berendes, Publishing Director

Editorial Directions, Inc.: E. Russell Primm, Editor; Alice Flanagan, Photo Researcher; Linda S. Koutris, Photo Selector; The Design Lab, Designer and Page Production; Red Line Editorial, Fact Researcher; Irene Keller, Copy Editor; Tim Griffin/IndexServ, Indexer; Donna Frassetto, Proofreader

Copyright © 2003 by The Child's World®
All rights reserved. No part of this book may be reproduced or utilized in any form or by any means without written permission from the publisher.

Library of Congress Cataloging-in-Publication Data
Gray, Shirley W.
 Living with diabetes / by Shirley Wimbish Gray.
   v. cm.— (Living Well series)
Includes index.
Contents: Do you know someone who has juvenile diabetes?—What is diabetes?— What's it like to have diabetes?—What can we do about diabetes?—Who gets diabetes?
 ISBN 1-56766-102-5
 1. Diabetes—Juvenile literature. 2. Diabetes in children—Juvenile literature.
[1. Diabetes. 2. Diseases.] I. Title. II. Series.
 RC660.5 .G73 2002
 618.92'462—dc21   2002002868

TABLE OF CONTENTS

AUG 0 5 2004

CHAPTER ONE

DO YOU KNOW SOMEONE WHO HAS JUVENILE DIABETES?

The crowd cheered when Gary Hall Jr. pulled himself out of the swimming pool. He had just won a gold medal at the 2000 Olympic Games. His body was tired, but Gary was happy.

Some people had thought Gary could not win a gold medal. They thought he should not even try, because Gary has Type 1 diabetes (dy-uh-BEET-uhs). Training for the Olympics could be bad for his body. But Gary read all about diabetes and learned how to take care of his body. He did what his doctor told him to do. He did not let diabetes stop him from reaching his goal.

By the time the Summer Olympics ended in Sydney, Australia, Gary had won four medals. He earned two gold, one silver, and one bronze. The newspapers called him the world's fastest swimmer.

Maybe you know somebody who has Type 1 diabetes. Or maybe you have it yourself. Type 1 diabetes is also called juvenile (JOO-vuh-nuhl) diabetes. About 1 child in every 600 has it. Learning about Type 1 diabetes is one way to help children who have it. Then they can reach their goals like Gary did.

Gary Hall Jr. receives one of his Olympic medals for swimming during an award ceremony in Sydney, Australia.

CHAPTER TWO

WHAT IS DIABETES?

Your body needs energy so that you can grow and play. Most of the food you eat gets broken down into glucose (GLOO-kohs). Glucose is a type of sugar found in the blood. It teams up with a hormone called insulin. Insulin is made in the pancreas (PAN-kree-uhs), a large organ near your stomach. Insulin helps the glucose get into cells so that your body can use the glucose as fuel. Then

Glucose gives the body energy for growing and playing.

you have energy for playing kickball or doing schoolwork.

Usually, the **immune system** protects the body from disease. But in Type 1

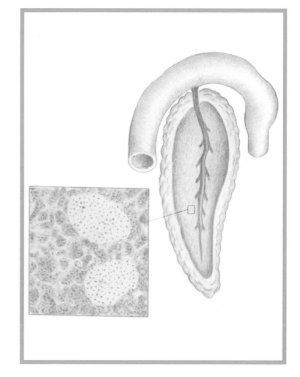

An illustration of the pancreas

diabetes, the **beta cells** of the pancreas do not work properly. In children with diabetes, the immune system attacks the beta cells in the body. Without them, the pancreas makes little or no insulin. As a result, glucose cannot get into the cells. Instead, the glucose builds up in the blood and some of it spills into the **urine.** Then the glucose passes out of the body as waste and the body does not get the fuel it needs for energy.

No one can see that the immune system has started attacking the beta cells, so it may go on for several years. In time, the beta cells of the pancreas no longer make insulin. Then the body begins showing **symptoms,** or signs, of diabetes.

One sign of diabetes is getting very thirsty and needing to go to the bathroom often. Another symptom is being hungry all the time, yet losing weight. Children who develop diabetes may also feel very tired because their bodies are not getting the fuel they need.

One of the symptoms of diabetes is being very thirsty and needing to go to the bathroom a lot.

CHAPTER THREE

WHAT'S IT LIKE TO
HAVE DIABETES?

A doctor does tests to find out if a child has diabetes. Children

who develop Type 1 diabetes will have it all their lives. The good

news is that they can learn how to take care of their condition.

Doctors and nurses, families and

teachers can help them.

Friends can be the

biggest help of all.

Children

with diabetes

must plan what

they will eat each day.

They must also plan

An insulin bottle and syringe

when they will eat. They cannot skip a meal or their blood sugar gets too low. Eating small healthy snacks during the day helps keep their blood sugar at a normal level.

Running and playing help keep sugar at a normal level, too. Playing on a soccer team or shooting hoops with friends are great things to do. So are riding bikes or going skating. You can help a

Getting lots of exercise, such as playing soccer, is a good way to keep sugar levels normal.

*Eating a healthy breakfast first thing in the morning helps
bring sugar levels back up to normal levels.*

friend who has diabetes just by playing together.

Sometimes living with Type 1 diabetes is hard. Teenagers with Type 1 never get to sleep late on Saturdays. Sugar levels may drop during the night. Most people with diabetes check their sugar level as soon as they wake up. Then they eat breakfast. That way, their bodies get the fuel they need.

Eating treats such as cake and ice cream is okay with some planning.

Going to a friend's birthday party can be hard, too. Cake and ice cream raise sugar levels. But with good planning, a child with diabetes can have a good time. People with diabetes can take insulin to help keep their sugar levels normal. If a child knows they will be eating cake at a party, he or she might take extra insulin before arriving. After eating the cake, everyone might play an active game, and the child who has diabetes can have as much fun as everyone else.

CHAPTER FOUR

WHAT CAN WE
DO ABOUT DIABETES?

Insulin was discovered in 1921. Before that, most people with Type 1

diabetes died soon after they

became ill. Now people

with diabetes can have long,

healthy lives. They do this

by keeping their blood-

glucose level as normal as

possible. They also take

insulin and they exercise.

People with Type 1

diabetes get insulin every

day. Most people do this by

Healthy, balanced meals help keep
blood-glucose levels normal.

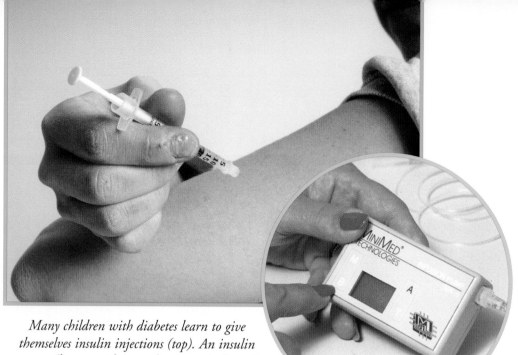

Many children with diabetes learn to give themselves insulin injections (top). An insulin pump (bottom right) supplies a steady flow of insulin as the patient needs it.

injection (in-JEK-shuhn). That means

they get a shot of insulin. It's like getting a flu shot. Some children

who have diabetes inject themselves with insulin two, three, or four

times a day.

Many children use insulin pumps so that they do not need

injections. The pump sends insulin through a small catheter, or

tube, that has been placed under the skin. That way, the child

gets a steady supply of insulin all day.

People with diabetes also need to know how much sugar is in their blood. To find out, they check their blood many times each day. Most children with diabetes even check their blood sugar while they are at school.

To do the check, the child puts a drop of blood from a finger on a special test strip. Then a small machine called a glucose meter reads the strip. The meter records how much sugar is

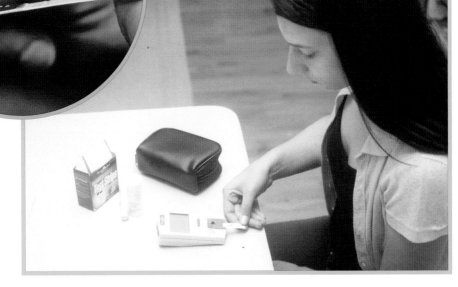

A drop of blood is placed on a special test strip (top). Then the strip is inserted into the glucose meter to find out blood-glucose levels (bottom).

Fruit juice not only tastes great, it can help raise blood-glucose levels quickly.

in the child's blood.

Low blood sugar is the most common problem in children who have diabetes. With low blood sugar, a child may have shaky hands and start sweating. Sometimes, low blood sugar causes a child to be sleepy.

Drinking fruit juice is one way to raise the sugar level.

Too much sugar in the blood is also dangerous. Children with high blood sugar may be very thirsty or tired and have to go to the bathroom more frequently. If this happens, a child may take some extra insulin.

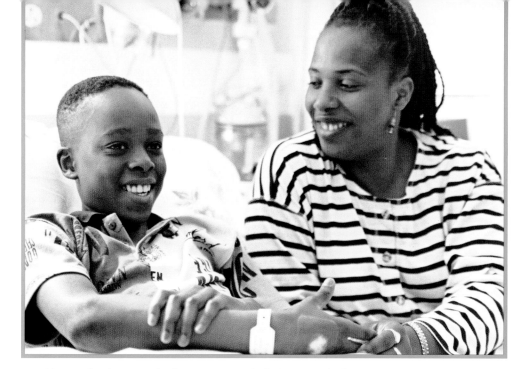

If ketone levels get too high, a person with diabetes might have to get help at a hospital.

If the body does not have glucose to burn as fuel, it may start burning stored fat. Then, **ketones** could build up in the child's body. High levels of ketones in the blood and urine can make a child very sick.

The breath of a child with high ketone levels may smell fruity. The child may also be tired, or have trouble breathing, or even throw up. Medical help is needed right away. Without it, the child could go into a **coma.**

CHAPTER FIVE

WHO GETS DIABETES?

Nicole Johnson is a former Miss America. Kelli Kuehne is a

professional golfer. Jay Leeuwenburg plays professional football.

*Professional golfer Kelli Kuehne has
Type 1 diabetes.*

Guess what these three people have in

common! They all have Type 1 diabetes.

Type 1 diabetes can develop at any

age, but it is most common in children

and young adults. No one knows why

the body's immune system begins

attacking its beta cells. Scientists think a

person's **genes** may be part of the

problem. Viruses may also be involved.

Sometimes several people in one

family may get diabetes. Type 1 diabetes is most common in people who are white. It is rare in people whose **ancestors** came from Africa or Asia. It is also rare in children from Native American families. No one knows the reason for this.

You might have a grandmother who has diabetes. If so, she may

Chris Dudley started playing basketball in the sixth grade. When he was 16, he learned that he had Type 1 diabetes. The first thing he asked was whether he could keep playing basketball. The answer was yes. Today, Dudley is one of the best defensive players in the National Basketball Association. Now he teaches children with diabetes to play basketball. He also teaches them about their disease. He thinks basketball is a great way to stay active!

Type 2 diabetes doesn't usually occur until a person is at least 40 years old.

have Type 2 diabetes. In people with Type 2, the pancreas does not make enough insulin. Or the pancreas may make enough, but the body does not use it properly.

Most people are at least 40 years old before they develop Type 2 diabetes. This form of the disease is common in African-American and Native American adults. Many people with Type 2 are overweight. Sometimes they have to inject themselves with insulin. Usually, they can control their disease by eating the right foods. They can also take a pill that helps their bodies. In recent years, more children and young adults have been diagnosed with Type 2 diabetes. Many experts believe this is because today's children

Adults and children have seen Mary Tyler Moore on TV for years. Now they watch her work for a cure for diabetes. This famous actress developed Type 1 diabetes more than 30 years ago. In June 2001, she went to Washington, D.C., and spoke to a group of senators. She told them, "Diabetes changes everything about a child's and a family's everyday life." She thinks scientists can find a cure for diabetes, so she asked the lawmakers to give more money to diabetes research.

Type 2 diabetes is more common in African Americans and Native Americans.

spend more time watching TV and less time playing active games and

sports. More children are overweight because they don't get enough

exercise, and being overweight is a risk factor for Type 2 diabetes.

Sometimes women develop diabetes while they are pregnant. This is called gestational (jeh-STAY-shuhn-al) diabetes. After the baby is born, the mother's diabetes usually goes away. However, the mother may develop Type 2 diabetes when she is older.

Sometimes pregnant women develop a form of diabetes called gestational diabetes.

CHAPTER SIX

WILL WE EVER
CURE DIABETES?

Children with Type 1 diabetes work hard to keep normal sugar

levels. But even with the right levels, they have a somewhat higher

risk of certain health problems. Over a long period of time, some

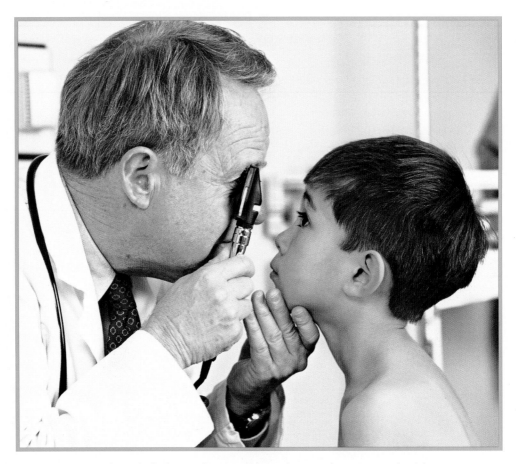

People with diabetes take extra care to be sure their eyes are healthy.

people with diabetes develop problems with their eyesight. Others might develop heart or kidney problems. Many have problems with wounds that heal slowly or not at all. Sometimes people die because of problems caused by this disease.

We have no cure for diabetes yet. Scientists still have lots of questions to answer. Why does the immune system attack the beta cells? Can the body make new beta cells? Is there an easier way to get insulin into the body? How can we protect the heart and the kidneys from damage?

Scientists have some clues. For example, our genes may play a part. If so, then the brothers and sisters of a child with Type 1 could be tested. This could help doctors find out who else might develop diabetes.

Doctors have also tried transplanting the pancreas. This means they put in a new pancreas from a donor who died, or part of a pancreas from a living donor. They have also tried giving the pancreas new beta cells. Could this help the body make its own insulin again? Doctors do not know the answer yet.

There may be new ways to give the body insulin in the future. Maybe children will use an inhaler like people with asthma do. They may also be able to wear a patch. Then the body could get the insulin through the skin. Doctors also want to find new ways to test blood sugar levels.

Scientists and doctors need help answering these

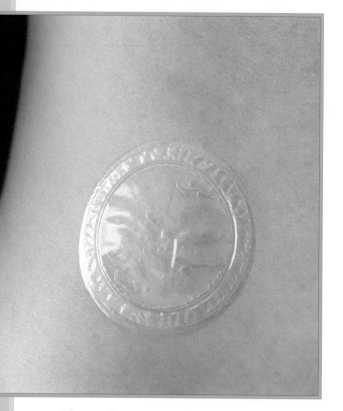

This patch contains insulin that is absorbed through the skin.

Sharing healthy snacks is one way to let a friend with diabetes know you care about them.

questions. Sometimes they ask people with diabetes to be in clinical trials. These are studies that test new ideas. People in clinical trials become part of the research team.

You can help, too. Do you know someone with Type 1 diabetes? If so, be a good friend. Invite your friend to play outdoors with you. Offer to share a healthy snack. Remind your friend to do a blood sugar check if you are on a field trip at school. Keeping sugar levels on target is not easy. Having a friend helps.

Glossary

ancestors (AN-sess-turs) Your ancestors are your relatives who lived long ago, such as your grandfathers and great grandfathers.

beta cells (BAY-tuh SELS) Beta cells are insulin-secreting cells in the pancreas.

coma (KOH-muh) A coma is a state of unconsciousness caused by an illness or injury to the body.

genes (JEENS) Genes are the part of a cell that decides which features of the parents a child will inherit.

immune system (ih-MYOON SISS-tuhm) The immune system protects the body from disease.

ketones (KEE-tohns) Ketones are the chemicals made when the body burns fat.

symptom (SIMP-tuhm) A symptom is a signal that the body is sick or injured.

urine (YOOR-uhn) Urine is the fluid containing waste that passes from the kidneys out of the body.

Questions and Answers about Diabetes

What is Type 1 diabetes? Type 1 diabetes is a disorder that keeps the body from using glucose for energy and growth. Type 1 diabetes is sometimes called juvenile diabetes.

Who gets Type 1 diabetes? Type 1 diabetes is usually seen in children and young adults. It is more common in white people whose families came from Europe. It is rare in people whose ancestors came from Africa or Asia or from Native American families.

How many people have it? More than 1 million people in the United States have Type 1 diabetes. More than 400,000 new cases are reported each year.

How is Type 1 diabetes treated? The treatment of Type 1 diabetes includes healthy eating, physical exercise, and injections of insulin.

Can I catch it? No, you cannot catch Type 1 diabetes the way you catch the flu or a cold, for example.

Will a child with diabetes ever get rid of it? No. Children who have this type of diabetes will have it for the rest of their lives, as far as we know.

Is there a cure for it? Not yet. Scientists are testing to see if they can give the body new beta cells or a new pancreas. If so, the body could begin to make insulin again. This could lead to a cure.

Helping a Friend Who Has Juvenile Diabetes

▶ Run, play ball, ride your bikes, or take a walk together. Exercise helps keep sugar levels in good ranges.

▶ Share healthy snacks, such as cheese and crackers, peanuts, pretzels, and fruit juice.

▶ Watch the clock and help your friend remember to test for blood sugar or take insulin.

▶ Tell an adult if your friend faints, has blurry vision, fruity-smelling breath, or trouble breathing. If you cannot find an adult, call 911.

Did You Know?

▶ Every year more than 13,000 American children are diagnosed with Type 1, or juvenile, diabetes. That's 35 children each and every day.

▶ Since its start in 1970, the Juvenile Diabetes Research Foundation has provided more than $500 million to diabetes research worldwide.

▶ More than 1 million Americans have Type 1 diabetes.

How to Learn More about Diabetes

At the Library: Nonfiction
Antoinette, Carol.
Sugar Was My Best Food.
Morton Grove, Ill.: Albert Whitman & Company, 1998.

Carter, Alden R., and Carol S. Carter (Illustrator).
I'm Tougher Than Diabetes.
Morton Grove, Ill.: Albert Whitman & Company, 2001.

Gordon, Melanie Apel.
Let's Talk about Diabetes.
New York: Rosen Publishing Group, 1999.

At the Library: Fiction
Beatty, Monica Driscoll, and Kathy Parkinson (Illustrator).
My Sister Rose Has Diabetes.
Albuquerque, N.M.: Health Press, 1997.

Betschart, Jean.
A Magic Ride in Foozbah-Land: An Inside Look at Diabetes.
New York: John Wiley & Sons, 1995.

Gosselin, Kim, and Terry Ravanelli (Illustrator).
Rufus Comes Home.
Valley Park, Mo.: JayJo Books, 1993.

Gosselin, Kim, and Moss Freedman (Illustrator).
Taking Diabetes to School.
Valley Park, Mo.: JayJo Books, 1998.

Mazur, Marcia L., Banks, Peter, and Andrew Keegan.
The Dinosaur Tamer and Other Stories for Children with Diabetes.
Chicago: Contemporary Books, 1995.

Mulder, Linnea.
Sarah and Puffle: A Story for Children about Diabetes.
New York: Magination Press, 1992.

Pirner, Connie White, and Nadine Bernard Westcott (Illustrator).
Even Little Kids Get Diabetes.
Morton Grove, Ill.: Albert Whitman & Company, 1994.

On the Web
Visit our home page for lots of links about diabetes:
http://www.childsworld.com/links.html

Note to Parents, Teachers, and Librarians: We routinely verify our
Web links to make sure they're safe, active sites—so encourage your
readers to check them out!

Through the Mail or by Phone
Alternativediabetes.com
2005 South 91st Street
Omaha, NE 68124
402/393-6391

American Association of Diabetes Educators
100 West Monroe Street, Suite 400
Chicago, IL 60603-1901
312/424 2426

The American Diabetes Association
1701 North Beauregard Street
Alexandria, VA 22311

Diabetes Public Health Resource
CDC Division of Diabetes Translation
P.O. Box 8728
Silver Spring, MD 20910
877/CDC-DIAB

Juvenile Diabetes Foundation International
120 Wall Street, 19th Floor
New York, NY 10005

Juvenile Diabetes Research Foundation International
120 Wall Street
New York, NY 10005-4001
800/533-CURE or 212/785-9500

The National Institute of Diabetes and Digestive and Kidney Diseases
Offices of Communications and Public Liaison
31 Center Drive, MSC 2560,
Bethesda, MD 20892-2560

Index

About the Author

Shirley Wimbish Gray has been a writer and educator for more than 25 years and has published more than a dozen nonfiction books for children. She also coordinates cancer education programs at the University of Arkansas for Medical Sciences and consults as a writer with scientists and physicians. She lives with her husband and two sons in Little Rock, Arkansas.